MINI MAKERS

Mini TREATS
TO ENJOY and SHARE

by Megan Borgert-Spaniol

a Capstone company — publishers for children

Raintree is an imprint of Capstone Global Library Limited, a company incorporated in England and Wales having its registered office at 264 Banbury Road, Oxford, OX2 7DY – Registered company number: 6695582

www.raintree.co.uk
myorders@raintree.co.uk

Hardback edition © Capstone Global Library Limited 2024
Paperback edition © Capstone Global Library Limited 2025
The moral rights of the proprietor have been asserted.

All rights reserved. No part of this publication may be reproduced in any form or by any means (including photocopying or storing it in any medium by electronic means and whether or not transiently or incidentally to some other use of this publication) without the written permission of the copyright owner, except in accordance with the provisions of the Copyright, Designs and Patents Act 1988 or under the terms of a licence issued by the Copyright Licensing Agency, 5th Floor, Shackleton House, 4 Battle Bridge Lane, London, SE1 2HX (www.cla.co.uk). Applications for the copyright owner's written permission should be addressed to the publisher.

Edited by: Jessica Rusick
Designed by: Aruna Rangarajan, Sarah DeYoung
Originated by Capstone Global Library Ltd

ISBN 978 1 3982 5167 0 (hardback)
ISBN 978 1 3982 5172 4 (paperback)

British Library Cataloguing in Publication Data
A full catalogue record for this book is available from the British Library.

Acknowledgements
We would like to thank the following for permission to reproduce photographs: iStockphoto: avean (font), Front Cover, 1, Back Cover; Mighty Media, Inc.: project photos; Shutterstock: Africa Studio, Front Cover (wooden stir sticks), 25 (oven mitt), Bozena Fulawka, Front Cover (cinnamon stick), Davydenko Yuliia, Front Cover (napkins), EKramar, 5 (spatula), Ground Picture, 5 (right), ifong, 13 (whisk), Kostikova Natalia, Front Cover (confetti), TabitaZn, Back Cover (gift tag), timquo, Front Cover (paper cup), tsingha25, Front Cover (bowl), VGstockstudio, 5 (left)

Design Elements: iStockphoto: Tolga TEZCAN; Shutterstock: ds_vector, Valerii_M

Every effort has been made to contact copyright holders of material reproduced in this book. Any omissions will be rectified in subsequent printings if notice is given to the publisher.

All the internet addresses (URLs) given in this book were valid at the time of going to press. However, due to the dynamic nature of the internet, some addresses may have changed, or sites may have changed or ceased to exist since publication. While the author and publisher regret any inconvenience this may cause readers, no responsibility for any such changes can be accepted by either the author or the publisher.

Printed and bound in India

CONTENTS

Mini treats 4

Mini ice lollies 6

Mini hot chocolate jar 8

Mini ice cream sandwich 10

Mini mug cake 12

Mini dessert tacos 14

Mini berry pies 16

Mini cheesecakes 18

Mini cinnamon rolls 20

Mini doughnuts 24

Mini layered cake 28

Find out more 32

About the author 32

MINI TREATS

There's nothing better than homemade treats to enjoy or give to others. The delicious desserts in this book are flaky, creamy, and best of all, mini! Are you in the mood for a tiny treat?

Bake a tray of **delicious doughnuts** or **snack-size cinnamon rolls**.

Keep cool with some **cute ice cream sandwiches** or the **ideal ice lollies**.

Or stir up a **mini microwavable cake** in an extra-small mug.

Whatever you choose, these mini treats will be perfect for you to **ENJOY** and **SHARE**!

BASIC SUPPLIES

- » baking tray
- » bowls
- » forks and spoons
- » measuring cups and spoons
- » muffin tray
- » plastic bags
- » rolling pin or glass jar
- » scissors
- » spatula
- » whisk

Crafting tips

SET YOURSELF UP FOR SUCCESS! Read through the ingredients and instructions before starting a project. Wipe down your work surface to make it clean before you begin to bake.

LET YOUR CREATIVITY SHINE! Put your own stamp on these recipes. Don't be afraid to make changes or try something new!

RECYCLE! Lots of the projects in this book use ingredients that come in plastic or cardboard packaging. Remember to recycle it!

ASK FIRST! Get permission from an adult to do the projects before you start baking.

SAFETY FIRST! Ask an adult for help with projects that require sharp cutlery or an oven.

CLEAN UP! When you've finished baking, make sure you put away any supplies you took out. Clean up any spills and wipe down your baking surface.

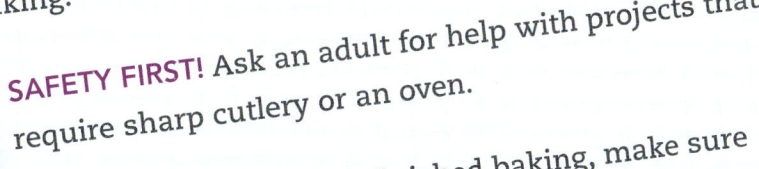

Mini ICE LOLLIES

These peaches-and-cream ice lollies are the perfect chilled treat for a hot day!

MATERIALS
- » whisk
- » tinned peaches
- » liquid measuring jug
- » vanilla yogurt
- » milk
- » ice cube tray
- » wooden lolly sticks
- » scissors
- » freezer

1

Use a whisk to mash 12 slices of tinned peaches in a liquid measuring jug. You should have about 175 grams of crushed peaches.

2

Combine the crushed peaches with 125 grams yogurt and 125 millilitres milk.

3

Divide the mixture evenly among the sections of the ice cube tray.

4

Insert a lolly stick into each section of the tray. Cut the stick in half if it is too long.

5

Place the ice cube tray in the freezer for about four hours or until the ice lollies are completely frozen. Enjoy!

TINY TIP
Try using different tinned or fresh fruit to make new lolly flavours!

Mini HOT CHOCOLATE JAR

MATERIALS

- » small bowl
- » whisk
- » measuring cups and spoons
- » powdered milk
- » sugar
- » cocoa powder
- » funnel or piece of paper
- » small jar with lid
- » mini marshmallows
- » coloured card or patterned paper
- » scissors
- » marker pen
- » hole punch
- » ribbon or string

Give this sweet single-serve hot chocolate mix to a friend and tell them to just add water!

1

In a small bowl, whisk together 30 grams powdered milk, 2 teaspoons sugar and 2 teaspoons cocoa powder.

2

Use a funnel or piece of rolled-up paper to pour the cocoa powder into the jar.

3

Top the mix with several mini marshmallows. Then screw on the lid.

4

Make a "Hot Chocolate for One" tag out of coloured card or patterned paper. Include the direction to add 175 ml of hot water.

5

Punch a hole in the tag. Tie the tag to the jar with ribbon or string. Gift the jar to a hot chocolate lover!

Mini ICE CREAM SANDWICH

MATERIALS

- » cookie dough
- » measuring spoon
- » baking tray with greaseproof paper
- » oven
- » freezer
- » tray or plate
- » ice cream scoop or spoon
- » vanilla ice cream
- » chocolate chips or sprinkles

Cookies or ice cream? You get both in a mini bite with this delicious treat!

1

Scoop ½ tablespoon of the cookie dough and roll into a ball. Repeat with the rest of the dough. If the dough is already divided, you can cut the portions to the size of your choice.

2

Place the dough balls on a baking tray lined with greaseproof paper. Bake according to the instructions on the package, reducing the baking time by a few minutes.

3

Once the cookies have cooled, place the baking tray in the freezer for 10 minutes. This will firm up the cookies.

4

Place the cookies on a tray or plate. Scoop vanilla ice cream onto the bottom of one cookie. Place a second cookie on top of the ice cream to form a sandwich. Repeat to make sandwiches out of the remaining cookies.

5

Cover the sides of the ice cream sandwiches in chocolate chips or sprinkles.

6

Place the tray or plate into the freezer until the ice cream sets. Eat your frozen treats on a warm day!

TINY TIP
If your ice cream is too hard, place it in the fridge for 15 minutes to soften.

Mini MUG CAKE

With a mini mug and a few basic ingredients, you're just 90 seconds away from yummy chocolate cake!

MATERIALS

- » small bowl
- » whisk
- » measuring spoons
- » self-raising flour
- » cocoa powder
- » sugar
- » baking powder
- » milk
- » vegetable oil
- » mini chocolate chips
- » microwave-safe espresso mugs
- » microwave
- » ice cream scoop or spoon (optional)
- » ice cream (optional)

1

In a small bowl, whisk together 1 tablespoon flour, ½ teaspoon cocoa powder, 1 tablespoon sugar and ¼ teaspoon baking powder.

2

Whisk in 30 ml milk, 15 ml vegetable oil and 1 tablespoon mini chocolate chips.

3

Divide the batter among two or three espresso mugs, filling each mug about halfway.

4

Microwave the mugs together on high for 90 seconds. Let the mugs and cake cool slightly.

5

If you like, top the mug cakes with small scoops of ice cream and more mini chocolate chips. Then dig in!

Mini DESSERT TACOS

Craft your own sweet tacos out of cinnamon-sugar shells and fruit filling!

MATERIALS

- » oven
- » cookie cutter or small glass
- » flour or corn tortillas
- » small bowl
- » measuring spoons
- » sugar
- » cinnamon
- » microwave-safe bowl
- » microwave
- » butter
- » spoon or pastry brush
- » muffin tray
- » strawberries
- » knife
- » whipped cream
- » mini chocolate chips

1

Preheat the oven to 190° Celsius. Use a cookie cutter or the rim of a small glass to cut the tortillas into mini tortillas.

2

In a small bowl, mix 10 grams sugar and 2.5 g cinnamon. Set the bowl aside.

3

Melt 15 g butter in a microwave-safe bowl. Use a spoon or pastry brush to spread the butter over both sides of each mini tortilla.

4

Cover the sides of each buttered tortilla with the cinnamon sugar mixture.

5

Flip the muffin tray upside down. Fold each mini tortilla and place it between two muffin cups so it stays folded.

6

Place the muffin tray in the oven and bake the mini tortillas for 12 to 15 minutes. The tortillas are ready if you slide them off the tray and they hold their taco shape.

7

While the tortilla shells cool on the tray, cut several strawberries into small cubes.

8

Fill each taco with strawberry cubes. Top the strawberries with whipped cream and mini chocolate chips!

Mini BERRY PIES

These sweet berry pies fit in the palm of your hand!

MATERIALS

- » oven
- » measuring jug and spoons
- » whisk
- » mixed berries
- » sugar
- » lemon juice
- » flour
- » shortcrust pastry (ready-made)
- » rolling pin or glass jar
- » cookie cutter or small glass
- » baking tray with greaseproof paper
- » fork
- » knife

1

Preheat the oven to 220°C. Use a whisk to mash 500 ml mixed berries in a liquid measuring jug. Add 25 g sugar and 15 ml lemon juice.

2

Roll out the pastry on a lightly floured surface. Use a cookie cutter or the rim of a small glass to cut out circles with a diameter of about 4 to 5 centimetres.

3

Place the circular cut-outs on a baking tray lined with greaseproof paper.

4

Scoop about 5 ml of the fruit mixture onto the centre of every other dough cut-out.

5

Place a plain pastry cut-out on top of the fruit pastry. Use the tines of a fork to seal the edges of the pie.

6

Use a knife to cut two or three small slits into the top of each pie.

7

Bake the mini pies for about 10 minutes or until they are golden brown. Let the pies cool before eating!

Mini CHEESECAKES

Use your favourite cookies as a crust for these tiny cheesecakes!

MATERIALS

- » cream cheese
- » measuring cups and spoons
- » sour cream
- » egg
- » oven
- » muffin tray with 6 cups
- » paper cases for muffin tray
- » biscuit of your choice
- » electric mixer
- » large bowl
- » sugar
- » vanilla extract
- » spatula
- » fridge
- » whipped cream

1

Put out 225 grams cream cheese, 80 g sour cream and 1 egg so they come to room temperature. This will help make the cheesecake creamy.

2

Preheat the oven to 180°C. Line the muffin tray with paper cases. Place a biscuit in each case.

3

Use an electric mixer to beat the cream cheese in a large bowl. Mix in 80 g sugar until the mixture is smooth.

4

Mix in the egg and 2.5 ml vanilla extract until everything is just combined. Use a spatula to stir in the sour cream.

5

Divide the batter between the muffin cases, filling each one with about 2 tablespoons of batter.

6

Bake the cheesecakes for 15 to 18 minutes. The cheesecakes should appear set but still jiggle a bit.

7

Let the cheesecakes cool completely. Then place them in the fridge for about two hours to chill.

8

Top each cheesecake with whipped cream and some crumbled biscuits.

Mini CINNAMON ROLLS

Bake some teeny weeny cinnamon rolls in a mini muffin tray!

MATERIALS

- » oven
- » croissant dough
- » baking tray
- » flour
- » rolling pin or glass jar
- » small bowls
- » measuring spoons
- » sugar
- » cinnamon
- » microwave-safe bowl
- » butter
- » microwave
- » spoon or pastry brush
- » knife
- » mini muffin tray with 12 cups
- » oil (optional)
- » fork
- » icing sugar (optional)

1

Preheat the oven to 190°C. Unroll the croissant dough onto a baking tray and sprinkle the dough with a pinch of flour.

2

Use a rolling pin or glass jar to flatten the dough to about 0.5 cm thick.

3

In a small bowl, mix 60 g sugar and 15 g cinnamon.

4

Melt 60 g butter in a microwave-safe bowl. Use a spoon or pastry brush to spread the melted butter evenly over the pastry rectangle.

5

Sprinkle the cinnamon and sugar over the pastry. With a spoon, spread the mixture evenly.

6

Roll up the pastry from one long end to the other to form a tube.

7

Use a knife to slice the dough into 12 equal pieces.

8

Grease the mini muffin cups with butter or oil. Place one pastry piece, swirl side up, into each muffin cup.

9

Bake the mini rolls for 15 to 18 minutes. When the pan cools, use a fork to carefully loosen each mini roll from the pan.

10

If you like, mix 50 g icing sugar with 7.5 ml water to make icing. Drizzle it over the rolls. Have your rolls for breakfast, dessert or a snack!

> **TINY TIP**
> If you want your icing to be thicker, add more icing sugar. If you want it to be runnier, add more water.

Mini DOUGHNUTS

Mini doughnuts taste extra sweet when they come straight from the oven!

MATERIALS

- » oven
- » vegetable oil
- » muffin tray
- » tin foil
- » large bowl
- » whisk
- » packet cake mix
- » measuring cups and spoons
- » water
- » egg
- » large plastic bag
- » scissors
- » small bowl
- » icing sugar
- » vanilla extract
- » milk
- » sprinkles

1
Preheat the oven to 180°C. Grease the muffin tray with oil.

2
Roll a strip of tin foil into a tube. Place the foil upright in the centre of a muffin cup. Repeat with the remaining muffin cups. This creates doughnut-shaped moulds.

3
In a large bowl, whisk together packet cake mix, 235 ml water, 1 egg and 60 ml vegetable oil.

4
Pour the batter into a large plastic bag. Cut off the tip of one corner to create a piping bag.

5

Pipe the batter into the doughnut moulds so the moulds are a quarter full.

6

Bake the doughnuts for 12 to 15 minutes. Let them cool completely before removing them from the pan.

7

Carefully pull the tin foil out of the doughnuts.

8

In a small bowl, whisk together 125 g icing sugar, ½ teaspoon vanilla extract and 15 ml water until you have a smooth glaze.

9

Spoon the glaze over the cooled dougnuts.

10
Top the doughnuts with sprinkles for a pop of colour!

TINY TIP
Make extra batter to cook more batches of doughnuts. Or, use the batter for the next project!

Mini LAYERED CAKE

With cakes this small, everyone gets their own!

MATERIALS

- » packet cake mix and ingredients listed on box
- » measuring jug and spoons
- » large bowl
- » whisk
- » baking tray
- » butter or oil
- » oven
- » cookie cutter or small glass jar
- » tray
- » freezer
- » cardboard
- » scissors
- » vanilla icing
- » knife
- » plastic bag
- » food colouring
- » sprinkles
- » tweezers (optional)

1
Follow the instructions on the packet cake mix to prepare the cake batter in a large bowl.

2
Grease a shallow baking tray with butter or oil and pour the cake batter into it. The batter should be about 0.5 to 1.5 cm deep. Divide the batter among multiple trays if you need to.

3
Bake the cake at the temperature noted on the box. Check the cake after 15 minutes. Continue baking until the cake is slightly golden and springs back when you tap the top.

4

Let the cake cool completely.

5

Use a cookie cutter or the rim of a small glass jar to cut two or three circular pieces from the cake. Cut more if you want to make more than one mini cake.

6

Place the circular pieces on a tray and put it in the freezer for about an hour. This will make the cake layers easier to work with as you ice them.

7

Cut out a cardboard circle that is slightly bigger than the base of your mini cakes. Spread a dot of icing in the centre of the cardboard and place a cake on top of the icing.

8

Spread icing on top of the cake. Place another cake on top. Spread icing on top of the second cake.

9

If you'd like your cake to be taller, add one more layer of cake and icing. Then ice the sides. If at any point the cake is crumbling into the icing, put it back into the freezer for 15 minutes before continuing to ice the cake.

10

Put 15 g icing into a plastic bag with a drop of food colouring. Knead the bag until the colour is mixed in.

11

Cut the tip off one corner of the bag to create a hole for piping the icing. Use the piping bag to decorate the cake however you like.

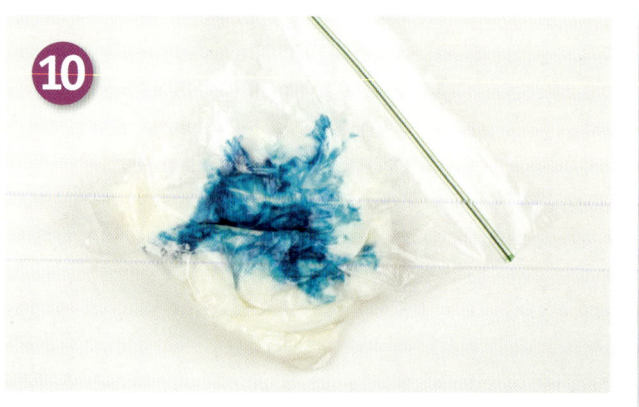

12

Add sprinkles to your cake. Use tweezers for precise placement!

FIND OUT MORE

BOOKS

10-Minute Crafty Projects (10-Minute Makers), Elsie Olson (Raintree, 2022)

Bake It: More Than 150 Recipes for Kids from Simple Cookies to Creative Cakes!, DK (DK Children, 2019)

Cooking Step By Step: More Than 50 Delicious Recipes for Young Cooks, DK (DK Children, 2018)

WEBSITES

www.bbc.co.uk/cbbc/curations/cbbc-recipes
Try some easy-to-make recipes featuring your favourite CBBC characters.

www.bbcgoodfood.com/recipes/collection/kids-dessert-recipes
Make some cakes and desserts using these BBC Good Food recipes.

www.cookingwithmykids.co.uk/cakes-and-cupcakes/
There are lots of cake recipes to make on this website.

ABOUT THE AUTHOR

Megan Borgert-Spaniol is an author and editor of children's media. When she isn't writing or reading, she enjoys doing yoga, eating croissants and making homemade pizzas. Megan lives in Minneapolis, Minnesota, USA, with a tall, goofy man and a small, chatty cat.